OPERATION "ALONE AT LAST"

I'm standing
near the children
watching them swarm
over the jungle gym,
remembering vaguely
what it was like to be six.

I'm stealing a glance at Dylan
as he ducks through the hole
in the chainlink fence
and disappears
into the sheltering darkness
of the woods.

I'm waiting,
just as we planned,
for my slow motion watch to tick off
three
full
minutes.

I'm sidling over
and sneaking through the same hole
into the shadows,
into the warm flanneled arms
of my partner
in delicious crime.

what my mother doesn't know

SONYA SONES

Simon Pulse
New York London Toronto Sydney

This book is a work of fiction. Any references to historical events, real people, or real locales are used fictitiously. Other names, characters, places, and incidents are the product of the author's imagination, and any resemblance to actual events or locales or persons, living or dead, is entirely coincidental.

First Simon Pulse edition February 2003
Copyright © 2001 by Sonya Sones

SIMON PULSE
An imprint of Simon & Schuster Children's Publishing Division
1230 Avenue of the Americas, New York, NY 10020

Also available in a Simon & Schuster Books for Young Readers hardcover edition.

Designed by Jennifer Reyes
Flip book by Sonya Sones
The text of this book was set in Tekton.

Printed in the United States of America
10 9 8 7 6 5 4 3 2 1

The Library of Congress has cataloged the hardcover edition as follows:
Sones, Sonya.
What my mother doesn't know / by Sonya Sones.
p.   cm.
Summary: Sophie describes her relationships with a series of boys as she searches for Mr. Right.
ISBN 0-689-84114-0 (hc)
[1. Dating (Social customs)—Fiction. 2. Love—Fiction.] 1. Title.
PZ7.S6978 Wh 2001
[Fic]—dc21
00-052634

ISBN 0-689-87114-7

ACKNOWLEDGMENTS

My heartfelt thanks to the generous women in my writing groups, Ruth Bornstein, Madeleine Comora, Ruth Feder, Peg Leavitt, Judith Pacht, Betsy Rosenthal, Hope Smith, Ann Wagner, and April Wayland, for all their terrific suggestions. A multitude of thank-yous to my oldest and dearest friend, Betsy Hochberg, for helping me to remember and to rediscover Boston. My deepest appreciation to my agent, Steven Malk, for pointing me towards the third act, and to my editor, David Gale, for trusting me to write it. And my undying gratitude to my own Mr. Right-and-a-Half, Bennett Tramer, for giving me, among many other precious gifts, my children.

For Ava and Jeremy—
I know *all*

what my mother doesn't know

NICKNAMES

Most people just call me Sophie
(which is the name
on my birth certificate),
or Sof,
or sometimes Sofa.
Zak and Danny think it's cute
to call me Couch,
as in:
"How're your cushions doing today, Couch?"
Or sometimes they call me Syphilis,
which I don't find one bit funny.
My parents usually call me
Sophie Dophie or Soso.
And Rachel and Grace call me Fifi,
or sometimes just Fee.

But Dylan calls me Sapphire.
He says it's because of my eyes.
I love the way his voice sounds
when he says it.
Sapphire.
I like whispering it to myself.
His name for me.
Sapphire.
It's like the secret password
to my heart.

Sixth Sense

Sometimes I just know things.
Like when Lou asked me to go on that walk
down by the reservoir last year
on the last day of eighth grade.
I knew he was going to say
he wanted to break up with me.

And I knew my heart
would shatter
when he did.

I just *know* things.
I can feel them coming.
Like a couple of weeks ago
when I went to the Labor Day party at Zak's.
Something perfect was going to happen.
I just knew it.

That was the night I met Dylan.

How It Happened

After Zak's party,
Rachel's big sister
came to drive a bunch of us home,
with her friend
and her friend's younger brother.

I was the last one to get in the car
and it turned out
all the other laps were taken,
so I had to sit on
Rachel's sister's friend's brother's lap.

It was
Dylan's lap,
but even though he goes to my school
I'd never seen him before.

And he had such smoldery dark eyes
that I felt like I'd been zapped
smack into the middle
of some R-rated movie
and everyone else in the car
was just going to fade away
and this guy and I
were going to start making out,
right then and there,

without ever having said
one word to each other.

But what really happened
was that he blushed and said,
"Hi. I'm Dylan."
And I blushed back and said,
"I'm Sophie."
And he said, "Nice name."
And I said, "Thanks."

After that we didn't say anything else
but our bodies seemed to be
carrying on a conversation of their own,
leaning together
into every curve of the road,
sharing skin secrets.

And just before we got to my house,
I thought I felt him
give my waist an almost squeeze.

4

Then the car rolled to a stop
and I climbed out
with my whole body buzzing.

I said good night,
headed up the front walk,
and when I heard the car pulling away,
I looked back over my shoulder
and saw Dylan looking over *his* shoulder
at me.

When our eyes connected,
this miracle smile lit up his face
and I practically had
a religious experience.

Then I went upstairs to bed
and tried to fall asleep,
but I felt permanently wide awake.
And I kept on seeing that smile of his
and feeling that almost squeeze.

Distracted in Math Class

All I have to do
is close my eyes

and I can feel his lips,
the way they felt
that very first time.

I can feel the heat of them,
parting just slightly,
brushing across my cheek,

moving closer
and closer still
to my mouth,

till I can hardly breathe,
hardly bear to wait
for them to press onto mine.

All I have to do
is close my eyes.

Between Classes with Dylan

We fall into step
in the crowded hall
without even glancing
at each other,

but his little finger
finds mine,
hooking us
together,

and all the clatter
of the corridor fades away
till the only sound I can hear
is the whispering of our fingers.

In the Cafeteria

Sitting alone
with Dylan.
Eating my sandwich,
but not
tasting it.

I'm only aware of
the sparks in his eyes,
the sun in his hair
and the spot where his knee's
touching mine.

Then, over his shoulder,
I see Rachel and Grace waving at me,
grinning like pumpkins,
holding up this little sign
with "Remember us?" written on it.

In the Girls' Bathroom

"Is he a good kisser?"
Rachel asks.
"Unbelievable," I say.

And it's true.
Dylan's kisses
seem like something
much *better* than kissing.

It's like
I can feel them
with my whole body.

That never used to happen
when Lou kissed me.
And he's the only other boy
I've ever made out with.

"Has he tried to get to second base?"
Grace wants to know.
But the bell rings just in time.

It's Been Rachel, Grace and Me Ever Since

That September afternoon,
when third grade had barely begun
and we were just getting
to know each other,
we skipped through
the first fallen leaves,
weaving our way through
the quiet neighborhood
to Sage Market for Häagen-Dazs bars.

That September afternoon,
when we saw the four older girls
pedaling towards us,
we didn't expect them to stop
or to leap off their bikes
and suddenly surround us.

But they did.

And we had no idea that the biggest one,
Mary Beth Butler,
who had these glinting slits for eyes,
would ask Rachel
what church she belonged to.

That September afternoon,
after Rachel mumbled, "Saint James's,"
we didn't know that Mary Beth
would ask Grace the same question,
or that Grace would squeak out,
"North-Prospect.
And it's none of your business."

But she did.

And when Mary Beth asked *me* the question
and I said I didn't go to church
because I was Jewish,
I didn't think she'd start shouting
at Rachel and Grace,
"Don't you know you aren't supposed
to play with anyone
who doesn't go to church?"
while her friends glared
and tightened their circle around us.

That September afternoon,
when Rachel kicked Mary Beth in the shin
and the three of us
crashed through the cage of bikes,
racing off together
across the nearest lawn,
scrambling through the hedge
and into the alley,
not stopping till we
were locked safely behind
the heavy oak of Rachel's front door,
we didn't know that we'd just become
best friends.

But we had.

WHY I DON'T MIND BEING AN ONLY CHILD

In fourth grade,
when Rachel had to put her dog to sleep,
we held a funeral for him
like the one Grace had seen
in Chinatown in San Francisco.

We marched down the middle of Meadow Way,
Rachel holding up a photo of Waggy,
Grace pounding solemnly on her snare drum,
me blasting out "The Dead Dog Blues"
on my clarinet.

In sixth grade,
when Grace's parents got divorced
during spring break,
we had a sleepover
that lasted three nights.

We painted Grace's nails Revenge Red,
covered her with henna tattoos,
watched a *Saved by the Bell* marathon,
and obliterated six pounds
of Oreo cookies.

Last June, when Lou dumped me
for that awful Alison Creely,
Rachel and Grace
helped me make a voodoo doll
that looked almost as stupid as him.

We poked it with a hundred pins
and wrote him a letter
which included all the swear words
we had ever heard,
as well as a few that we just made up.

But we didn't mail it.
We burned it in the fireplace instead,
along with the voodoo doll.
Then they dragged me off
to see a movie.

Watching Murphy During Art Class

He is so homely,
so downright ugly
that none of the girls
even think about him.

He's too lowly,
too pitiful
to even bother
making fun of.

So something must be
very wrong with me,
because I want to kiss him.
I want to kiss him real bad,

even though his nose is crooked
and his ears are huge,
even though his hair's a mess
and his lips are tight and scared.

I want to kiss away
those circles under his eyes
that make him look like
he's never slept a second in his life.

And those arms of his
seem like they're just aching
to hold on to someone.
I wish I could let them hold on to me.

When no one was looking,
I'd walk up to him
and say, "Hey, Murph.
Would it be okay if I kissed you?"

And he'd look hurt
because he'd think I was joking
and he'd turn away
to hide his face,

but I'd touch his shoulder and
look at him with gentle misty movie eyes
and say, "Come on. I mean it.
I really want to."

And he'd look dumbstruck,
and all the gray
would fade out of his eyes
and this light would come into them

and his lips would look like
they were getting ready to smile and then,
before I had a chance to change my mind,
I'd kiss him.

And he'd wrap his skinniness around me
and his arms would be shaking,
and suddenly I'd feel all this love,
all this need pouring into me

right through his lips
into me
and it would feel great,
and I'd close my eyes to feel it better.

(Whoa.
I can't believe
I'm having this fantasy about Murphy,
when I'm so totally in love with Dylan!)

DURING HISTORY CLASS

How can I study
when my blood is pumping so loud
that I can't hear my own thoughts?

How can I read
when all the words
keep swirling around on the page?

How can I concentrate
on Ancient Babylonia
when Dylan's note is burning in my pocket?

His Note

I stand by my locker
waiting,
till the hall
is practically empty.

Then I slip his note
out of my pocket,
carefully unfold each crease,
and read:

 "You are the coolest girl
in the whole world.
(And probably even on Mars, too.)
Meet me near the hole in the fence
after school."

I fold it back up,
press it to my heart,
then slip it into my pocket
and sprint to French class.

I'll be late,
but it was
très
worth it.

Operation "Alone at Last"

I'm standing
near the children
watching them swarm
over the jungle gym,
remembering vaguely
what it was like to be six.

I'm stealing a glance at Dylan
as he ducks through the hole
in the chainlink fence
and disappears
into the sheltering darkness
of the woods.

I'm waiting,
just as we planned,
for my slow motion watch to tick off
three
full
minutes.

I'm sidling over
and sneaking through the same hole
into the shadows,
into the warm flanneled arms
of my partner
in delicious crime.

Every Day When I Get Home from School

I find televisions on in the living room,
the family room,
the kitchen,
and each of the bedrooms.
There's even a little teensy one on
in the bathroom.

My mother says
it's so she won't miss anything
when she's going around sweeping
and dusting and putting away laundry
and emptying out wastebaskets
and cooking.

Which is what she does all day long.
Except for when she's lying in bed
watching television.
That's where she is
every afternoon
when I get home from school.

She glances up and says hello,
then goes back to watching.
I walk from room to room

switching off all the other sets,
wishing she would show
half as much interest in *my* life

as she does in Luke and Laura's.

HER SOAPS

My mother says
they keep her company.
But it's just the opposite for me.

Listening to that music
that swells up in the background
whenever someone announces they're pregnant
or dies of a drug overdose
or maybe finds out
their husband is having an affair
with their best friend's
stepsister's daughter-in-law,
makes me feel lonelier
than when I was little
and my mother used to
make me wait for her in the car
while she did her errands.

I used to be so scared
that the car would roll away.
So scared that my mother
would never come back.

Sometimes,
when she's watching her soaps,
it feels like she never did.

MAYBE DAD LOVES ME

But it's sure hard to tell.
I don't think he's ever
kissed me or hugged me
in his life.

Sometimes *I* hug *him*
but he doesn't hug me back.
His body just goes all stiff,
almost like he's scared of being touched.

Sometimes he jokes around
by putting his palms on my cheeks
and then leaning in
and kissing the back of each of his hands.

When I was real little,
he used to hold his long arm out straight
and put his hand
on my forehead.

Then he'd challenge me
to try to reach his body
with my short arms.
And of course I never could.

He seemed to think this was a riot
and I used to laugh right along with him,
but secretly I wished
he'd cut out the stupid game and hold me.

Dad's not that way though.
Even before they started fighting,
I never saw him touch Mom.
Not even to hold her hand.

I guess he's just not
the affectionate type.
And come to think of it,
neither are his parents.

Maybe it's hereditary or something.
I sure hope *I'm* not going to be like that.
But judging from how hard it is
for me to keep my hands off Dylan,

I seriously doubt it.

During Lunch

We're
searching the campus,
hand glued to hand,
hip glued to hip,

looking for a place
behind every hedge,
for just one small
and private spot

where we
can be alone
long enough
to do the serious kissing

that we absolutely
can't live without
for one more
minute.

Art Class

Mr. Schultz
has us building
found-art sculptures
with all this trash we gathered
from under the bleachers
next to the football field

and I'm so into it
that until the bell rings
I don't even notice
that I haven't
thought about Dylan once
for the entire forty-eight minutes.

I think I just set
my new world record.

SECRET SHELF

I'm rifling through the dust and jumble
of my parents' walk-in closet,
searching for the perfect belt
to wear with my new blue skirt,

when I happen to glance up
and see a small shelf
above the door
crammed with paperback books.

Strange to think that
I've been in this closet
hundreds of times before
and never once noticed it till now.

I pull over the chair
from my mother's dressing table,
climb up to take a closer look,
and just about faint:

here are some of
the dirtiest books
I've ever seen
in my life.

I try to picture
my mother and father
sitting around reading them,
but it's just too gross

and I suddenly realize
that I'll never be able
to think of my parents
in quite the same way as I used to

and that every time they go out
and leave me alone in the house,
I'll be racing right back up here
to grab another one off the shelf.

MOM AND DAD USED TO BE IN LOVE

Way back in the beginning anyhow.
I know because I can see it in their eyes
when I watch the old home videos
of when I was a baby.

They were *really* in love,
like people in the movies.

But now they have
these hideous battles all the time.
They scream their guts out
at each other about things like
how they should be raising me
or about money or the in-laws
or even just what movie to go see.

Their shrieking whips around inside me
like a tornado.
And no fingers crammed in my ears,
no pillows held over my head,
can block it out.

It makes me want to throw on my coat
and rush over to Rachel's
or to Grace's.

But I can't bring myself
to set foot outside.

What would I do if
I ran into one of the neighbors?

A neighbor who's heard
every
single
foul-mouthed word?

I've Got This Problem with Crying

Once I start,
I can't stop.

And what makes it so awful is
that if I cry any longer
than five minutes
(which of course I always do)
my eyes swell up like a boxer's
for at least twenty-four hours.

I've tried ice packs.
I've tried the cold cucumber cure.
I've even tried raw steak.
But nothing works.
Ever.

So when I've been crying,
I pray for sunshine
because if it's cloudy out
everyone keeps asking me
why I'm wearing my sunglasses,
and I get so embarrassed
that I start to cry,

and once I start,
I can't stop.

DINNER DOWNER

Seems like Dad's been going
on more and more business trips lately.
And when he's not out of town,
he's at his office twelve hours a day.

But once in a while
he makes it home by six
and the three of us have dinner together,
almost like a regular functional family.

We sit down at the kitchen table,
Dad flicks on the TV,
and we watch the evening news
while we eat.

Sometimes
I wish
I could just
switch it off,

so we could actually make
dinner conversation,
like they do over at Rachel's house,
and at Grace's.

Every now and then,
during the commercials
Dad will say something like,
"How was school today, Sophie Dophie?"

Once I said, "We played strip poker
during third period and I lost."
Dad just said, "That's nice,"
without even looking up from his meatloaf.

Lately, I've been trying
to concentrate on Dylan during dinner.
On imagining we're at Miss Mae's Diner.
Just the two of us.

It helps a little.

At Miss Mae's Diner

tucked in the corner
of our favorite booth

next to each other
instead of across

I'm trying hard to focus
on reading the menu

but his hand has slipped
under the tablecloth

and his fingers
are stroking my knee

DYLAN AND I BUMP INTO HIS OLD GIRLFRIEND AT THE MALL

She's
batting her lashes at him,
touching his arm,
saying how great he looks
and calling him Pickle, as in Dill. Ha. Ha.

He's
blushing and
flashing her these intimate grins,
as though her calling him that stupid name
is bringing back all these
secret fond memories.

And I'm
just standing here
with this paralyzed smile on my face,
wishing I could grab his hand
and make a dash for the elevator.

By Comparison

Watching Dylan
with his old girlfriend Ivy
makes me feel
like I'm some sort of
Amazonian freak of nature,
like I'm the Mount Everest
of teenage girls.

I bet whenever they went to the beach
he used to pick her up
and throw her in the water.
I bet if he tried to pick *me* up
his knees would buckle.
Not that I'm fat.
It's just that I'm tall
and there's so darn *much* of me.

I'm thinking
Dylan should be with someone
more like Ivy,
someone petite and blonde
and infinitely perky.
I'm wondering what he's doing
with huge old, mousy brown,
terminally sluggy me.

But when she finally wiggles away,
Dylan turns to me and says,
"Man, I used to hate it
when she called me Pickle.
And I forgot how tiny she was.
How could I ever have gone out
with someone who looks like
she could be my baby sister?"

Wow.
He always says
just
the right thing.
How does he do that?
I'm the luckiest
fifty-foot woman alive.

In English Class

If Mrs. Livingston glances up
from the stack of essays she's slashing
with her famous red pen,
it will appear as if I'm reading
The Grapes of Wrath.

But if she comes around
to look over my shoulder,
she'll catch me
staring at the photo
I've tucked into the center of the book,

the one
that Dylan slipped into my pocket
last night
just before
we kissed goodbye,

where he's
standing on the beach
with this surfer boy smile on his lips,
the wind tossing his blond curls
everywhere,

the one that says:
"for Sapphire
from a secret admirer"
inside a little heart
on the back,

the one where he looks so amazingly cute
that Mrs. Livingston might
just find herself
staring at him too,
instead of giving me detention.

During French Class

Je ne peux pas conjugate the verbs
parce que I'm sitting right across
from my old boyfriend Lou
and his lips.

I feel myself turning green
when I look at them:
thick, chapped,
gleaming under a drizzle of spit.

How could I *ever*
have let him kiss me?
I can even remember
wanting him to kiss me.

What could I have been thinking?

That mouth of his,
so perpetually overflowing
with saliva.
It *touched* mine.

Just last spring
that drooly tongue was in
my mouth.
More than once.

I think I'm gonna be sick.

Walking Home from School with Rachel and Grace

Listening to Grace moan about
how horny she is and about how if
she doesn't find a boyfriend soon
she's going to die of lackonookie disease,

and to Rachel complain about how
Danny can't take her out on Saturday night
because his parents have grounded him
again,

I see Murphy
trudging along up ahead
looking so immensely
alone

that I have to fight the urge
to run to catch up to him
and fill that huge empty space
by his side.

I'd never
be able to explain
a move like that
to Rachel and Grace.

Another Nuclear Meltdown

My parents just had
World War Twenty-seven.
Dad slammed out the door
and tore off in the car,
burning rubber like a thief
escaping from the scene of the crime.

Mom started bawling
and said that Dad
was a selfish son of a bitch
and that he makes her life miserable
because he doesn't give a damn
about her feelings.

She would have said
a whole lot more
but I told her I didn't want to hear it.
I said she ought to go see a therapist
if she was so unhappy,
and tell the *therapist* about it.

Mom said,
"If your *father* sees a therapist,
I'll be cured!"
I guess that just about
sums up her world view
in a nutshell.

Growing Up . . . and Out

My Aunt Betsy,
who lives in Hawaii,
has a bamboo forest growing in her backyard.

She says a bamboo stalk can grow
as much as four inches in a single day
and that if you sit there and watch it
you can actually see it getting taller.

Well, my breasts
have been growing
so fast lately

that if I were to sit there
and watch *them* for awhile,
I think I could actually
see them getting bigger.

Dylan hasn't said anything,
but I see him sneaking peeks
all the time.

It *is* pretty astonishing
how my molehills
have turned into mountains
overnight.

45

ICE CAPADES

Sometimes
on chilly nights
I stand close to my bedroom window,
unbutton my nightgown,
and press my breasts
against the cold glass
just so I can see
the amazing trick
that my nipples can do.

It's That Time of the Month Again

I wore
my brand-new white satin panties
to school today.

So,
naturally,
I got my period.

When Rachel gets hers,
she calls it riding the cotton pony.
Grace calls it surfing the crimson wave.

But I prefer
to think of it as
rebooting my ovarian operating system.

How My Mother Took the News

I remember how my mother reacted,
on that fateful day two years ago,
when I told her I'd gotten my first period:
her face turned the color of the ashes
dangling from the tip of her cigarette.

She tried to smile
but ended up looking like she just
took a gulp of
what she thought was water
only it turned out to be vinegar.

She rummaged around
in the bathroom cabinet
and handed me what I needed,
saying, "I've been keeping these for you.
For when the time came."

Then she patted me on the back,
looking like she wanted
to say something more.
But she didn't.
She just wandered out of the room,

leaving me with a box full of questions.

My First Time Buying You-Know-Whats

I had used my last one at school
right before lunch.
And I knew I didn't have
any more of them at the house,
so I stopped off on the way home
to buy some at Drugtown.

I wasn't too worried about it.
I figured I'd just cruise
down the feminine hygiene aisle
and act like I knew what I was doing.
Only I couldn't find the kind
my mother had been buying for me,
and I could not *believe*
how many different types of them
there were to choose from.

I finally made my decision
and headed to the cash register
with the neon pink cardboard box
tucked surreptitiously under my arm.

But I hadn't counted on a *guy*
being the cashier.
And I sure hadn't counted on that guy
being Rachel's cousin Perry,
on whom I had a severe crush.

I had to think fast.

So while he finished up
with the customer in front of me,
I managed to stash the box
behind an *Enquirer.*
Then, I bought a pack of Juicy Fruit
and got the heck out of there.

MOM'S THE WORD

My mother has never talked to me
about birth control or safe sex or about
whether I should wait till I'm married.

But whenever I'm getting ready
to go out with Dylan,
she hovers in the hall

and keeps wringing her hands,
like she's scared that
I'm going to get pregnant or something.

And if I ever did,
which of course I won't,
it would serve her right.

Actually, all we do so far is kiss
even though he wants to do more
and I won't let him.

But
I'm not about to
tell *her* that.

He'll Be Here Any Minute Now

and I'll watch him
from my bedroom window
when he hurries up the front walk
onto the porch

and he'll ring the bell
and my mother will answer the door
and he'll step into the hall
and they'll say hello to each other

and I'll come floating down the stairs
and his eyes
will singe my sweater
but my mother won't see

and we'll say goodbye to her
and head down the front walk
looking straight ahead
not even holding hands

feeling my mother's gaze
on our backs
and then we'll turn left
and go just a few more yards

and the second we're hidden
behind the Sweeneys' lilac hedge
we'll grab each other
and start kissing

In the Dark with Dylan

The truth is
I have no idea
what this movie's even about.

I couldn't tell the good guys
from the bad guys
if you paid me a million dollars.

But I *do* know
that there isn't anyone
on this whole entire planet

that I'd rather be
not watching this movie with
than Dylan.

CLOSE TO MIDNIGHT

Lying in bed
gazing up at the
glow-in-the-dark stars
on my ceiling,
I'm thinking of you

lying in bed
gazing up at *your* ceiling,
maybe thinking of me
at this very same
moment.

I'm thinking that
you've never seen my stars
glow in the dark,
and wondering
if you ever will.

Confession

All right.
I admit it.

When you aren't here,
I kiss my knee
and pretend it's you.

I know it's dumb.
But I do.

THE NAKED TRUTH

I can't even remember whose idea it was,
but we decided we were going to
do it!

So a few minutes ago,
Rachel and Grace and me
put on our raincoats
and walked over to Herrell's
for ice cream.

We couldn't stop giggling
the whole way over.

Now we're just sitting here,
eating our sundaes nonchalantly,
but Zak and Danny just came in.
And—oh no!
They're walking over to us!
We're nudging each other in the ribs,
trying hard not to crack up.

They want to know if they can sit with us!
I can feel my face catching fire.
But Rachel says we're having
a very private girl talk.
And Grace adds,
"Besides. This booth is too small.
There's *barely* enough room."

The three of us
burst into hysterics at this,
and Zak and Danny look at us
like they think we're nuts.

That's because
they don't know our secret:

This afternoon
before we put *on*
our raincoats,
we took everything else
off!

Left Out

Rachel and Grace
are sitting there on the bed,
laughing and chatting away,
taking turns
popping the zits
on each other's backs,

and I'm sitting here on the rug,
watching them,
feeling so left out
that I'm actually wishing
I had some zits
on my back, too.

Sick. Aren't I?

DYLAN'S BUZZ CUT

I wish he hadn't gone and cut his hair.
He looks about eight years old.
His ears have tripled in size.
Everyone's started calling him Dumbo.
Which wouldn't be so bad,
except they've started calling *me*
Mrs. Dumbo.

You can't even tell
he's got curly hair anymore.
There's nothing left
to run my fingers through.
Just this weird
blond AstroTurf
sprouting out of his skull.

FRIDAY NIGHT FIGHT

Dylan says he doesn't have
to ask for my permission
to get his hair cut.

I say I know
but maybe he could at least
warn me next time he's
planning on getting scalped.

And then he says it'll grow back
and I say it'll take forever
and then he says
he guesses I'll just
have to get used to it
and I say not if I don't
have to look at it anymore
and he says
you *don't!*

Then he stomps out of the house
and slams the door.
Loud.

And I kick it
so hard
that my dad has to get me some ice
to put on my big toe.

Long Weekend

Forty-eight hours
of silence go by.
Forty-eight hours
alone.
Forty-eight hours
is such a long time
to sit
and stare
at the phone.

I Didn't See Him at School Today

Not in the hall.
Not in the cafeteria.
Not in the library.
Not anywhere.
Not even once.

Not that I *wanted* to see him.
Not that I would have
said anything if I had.
Not that I would have run up to him
or flung my arms around him
or begged for forgiveness
or anything like *that*.

Well—
probably not.

I Yank Open the Door

And there he is.
But before he even has a chance
to say one word

I blurt out how sorry I am,
so sorry I wish I could go on national TV
and tell the whole world.

And he says he's so sorry
he wishes he could fill up my entire house
with roses.

And then I say I'm so sorry
I want to have it printed on
all the billboards in Massachusetts.

And then he says
he's going to have "I'M SORRY SAPPHIRE"
tattooed onto his chest.

And I say I'm going to hire
a thousand airplanes
to write it all over the sky.

And then he kisses me
and his I'm-sorry kisses are so sweet
that for a second

I find myself thinking
it was almost worth
having the fight.

I WISH

I wish I could drink a magic potion and
shrink way down till I was small
enough to fit right into his
shirt pocket and live
there tucked near to
his heart listening
to it beating in
rhythm with
mine every
minute of
every
day

I Loved Watching It Happen

The way his eyelids
got heavier and heavier.
The way his chin
drifted to his chest
and his history book
slipped into his lap.

I know I should be studying right now
but I can't resist
sketching him.

So until he wakes up,
I'm going to let my pencil trace
the contours
of his perfect cheekbones,
the shadows of his golden lashes,
the soft curve of his neck.

This
is definitely
bliss.

When Dylan Wakes Up

I show him
his portrait.

He glances at it
for a second,

then all he says
is "Cool."

The truth is,
Dylan doesn't *get* art.

But I guess
he doesn't have to.

He *is*
art.

The Meaning of Murphy

I don't know
how it got started,
but it happens
all the time:

When someone at school
acts like a dork
the other kids say,
"What a Murphy!"

Someone will do something dumb,
like today in science class
when Danny knocked a beaker onto the floor
and it crashed into a zillion pieces.

Zak shouted,
"Jeez, Danny!
Don't be such a Murphy!"
and the whole class burst out laughing.

(Okay.
I laughed too.
But only so no one would think
I was strange.)

I wonder how Murphy would feel
if he knew his name
had become synonymous
with "jerk."

I guess I *know* how he'd feel.

Art Class Exercise

Mr. Schultz says today we've got to sit
face to face with someone in class
and draw their portrait
while they draw ours.

I glance over at Murphy
and know
that if *I* don't choose him,
no one will.

So I do.

DRAWING EACH OTHER

He's drawing my nose.
I'm drawing his mouth.

He's drawing my mouth.
I'm drawing his nose.

He's drawing my eyes.
I'm drawing *his* eyes,

and suddenly I notice
that they're smiling into mine.

So I let my eyes
smile back at his,

and no one sees
but us.

I Show My Drawing to the Girls

Rachel just kind of gapes at it
and says, "Eeeeooooo.
You drew Murphy!"

I say, "No, duh."

Grace says, "You've captured
the utter Murphyness of Murphy,
you Murphy."

Rachel says, "Takes one to draw one."

And I clonk them both
over their heads
with my sketchbook.

Culture Clash

Dylan says
when I meet his mother today
I shouldn't mention
that I'm Jewish.

I say
okay, but can I
tell her about
the HIV positive thing?

He gives me a look.
I give him one back.

On the Way to Meeting Dylan's Mother

I'm thinking about the time
my mother and I were in the car,
waiting for an old lady who was taking forever
to pull out of a parking space
in front of Flair Cleaners.

I'm thinking about how when she finally drove off
this crow-faced man zipped
right into the space from behind us
and about how my mother
rolled down her window and said, "Excuse me, sir.
But we've been waiting
for that spot for five minutes."

I'm remembering what the man said
as he shoved open his car door:
"God damn kikes!"

I'm remembering
the look on my mother's face,
the way her hand flew up to her cheek,
as though she'd been slapped.

And I'm remembering
the first thought that came into my head:

Do we look *that* Jewish?

It's Just an Expression

Dylan's mother
is in the middle of having a garage sale
when we walk up.

She kisses him on the cheek,
and then starts pumping my hand,
saying how delighted she is
to finally be meeting me.

She says she only wishes
we'd been here this morning
because she could have used our help when
the huge crowd of "early birds" descended.

She says they were
swarming all over her stuff like flies
and everyone kept trying to
Jew her down on the prices.

I glance over at Dylan
to see his reaction to what she's said.
He just laughs and says, "That's how
people *are* at garage sales, Mom."

I don't know which is worse—
the fact that she said it,
or the fact that it didn't even faze him.

GRACE IS IN LOVE

For the past two weeks,
Grace hasn't stopped blabbing
to Rachel and me about
this new guy named Henry
who sits two seats over from her
in science class.

She says he's the most gorgeous creature
that she's ever laid eyes on
and she keeps telling us all about
how brilliant and hilarious he is,
and how he's got this English accent
that just about makes her drool.

And she says every time
she sneaks a glance at him,
she catches him staring at her
with this perfect little crooked smile,
and then he winks at her.
He actually *winks*.
And she just about dies
whenever he does that.

And she says he finally asked
for her phone number yesterday
and when he called her last night
she just about fainted
and they talked for three solid hours,
and she can't believe
how much they have in common.
They even have the same number
of letters in their names,
and she says he better ask her out soon,
because she doesn't think
she can go on like this
much longer.

He *better.*
Because we don't think
we can
either.

When We're Alone

Rachel does her Grace impression:
". . . He's got this Pig Latin accent
that just about makes me ool-dray.
And we have so much in common.
We even have the same number of zits!"

When she finishes,
we share a guilty giggle fit,
but then Rachel's smile fades
and she says sometimes
listening to Grace
go on and on about Henry
makes her feel as if
her relationship with Danny
is inferior or something.

She says she can't remember
ever having talked on
the phone with Danny
for more than twenty minutes
at a stretch.

Not even in the very beginning.

And when she says this,
I suddenly realize
that the same thing's true
about Dylan and me.

And my heart
sinks
all the way to China.

At the County Fair

If only
Dylan liked
Ferris wheels.

If only
I liked
roller coasters.

If only
Dylan liked
fun houses.

If only
I liked
bumper cars.

If only
Dylan liked
horse shows.

If only
I liked
video arcades.

If *only*
I had come with Rachel and Grace
instead.

Test Results Are In

I took one of those
really stupid magazine tests just now.

The kind that's supposed to tell you
how compatible you are with your mate.

This one was called:
"Is Your Mr. Right, Mr. Wrong?"

If you scored in the nineties
he was definitely Mr. Right.

Above seventy-five meant he was Mr. Maybe.
Above fifty meant he was Mr. Maybe Not.

And anything below fifty meant—
Well, *you* know.

I answered all those idiotic questions
as honestly as I could.

I *should* have lied.

I Don't Get It

I used to think it was so cute
the way Dylan's sneakers always
squeaked when he walked.

I liked teasing him about them.
Called them his squeakers.
Loved being able to hear
him coming a mile away.

When I'd hear that squeak of his
heading in my direction,
my heart would dance right up
into my throat.

I used to feel like I was floating
a few inches above the ground
whenever he was squeaking along
next to me.

But now when I hear those
noisy Nikes of his,
I feel like
I want to scream.

I want to stomp on his toes.
I want to trip him up and run away.
I just don't get it.

HE CALLS HIMSELF CHAZ

I like the ring of it—
chatting with Chaz.
I met him on the Internet last week
and we just seemed to click right away.
No pun intended.

We've been getting together
every night since then at ten o'clock
for these long private talks.
Just the two of us
floating through cyberspace.

There's something so neat
about not even knowing
what he looks like.
Something even neater
about not even caring.

And knowing
that *he* doesn't care
what *I* look like either.
It's a *soul* thing,
with us.

A cybersoul thing.

I made up that word.
Chaz really likes it.

MY MORAL DILEMMA

I ask Rachel and Grace
if they think it's the same thing
as cheating on Dylan
when I chat with Chaz.

Grace says that depends
on who I like talking to more,
the cyberstud (as she calls him)
or Dylan.

Grace says she can't imagine
wanting to talk to another guy
more than her new boyfriend Henry.
On the Net or otherwise.
She says it's a bad sign if
I don't feel that way about Dylan.

But Rachel says one person
can't completely fulfill
anybody's needs a hundred percent
and it's not as if
I'm actually *dating* Chaz,
so she doesn't see anything wrong with it.

I love that girl.

CYBER SOUL MATE

It's almost ten o'clock.
I can hardly wait
to see his voice.

His Words Pop Onto My Screen:

"So tell me about your day.
I want to know everything that happened
from the minute you woke up this morning
to right now."

I don't think anyone's
ever
been this interested in me before.
Not even *me*.

As I place my fingers
to the keys
and begin,
my heart does the happy chatroom dance.

More or Less

If Dylan and I had met
by chatting on the Net
in a room in cyberspace
instead of face to face
and I hadn't seen his lips
or the way he moves his hips
when he does that sexy dance
and I hadn't had a chance
to look into his eyes
or be dazzled by their size
and all that I had seen
were his letters on my screen,
then I might as well confess:
I think I would have liked him

less.

Double Date

All Grace has to do is smile at him
and Henry forgets what he's saying
right in the middle of his sentence.

And when he *can* complete a thought,
Grace acts like it's just about
the funniest thing she's ever heard.

Henry keeps wrapping
the little curl at the nape of her neck
around his finger,

and he hasn't let *go* of her hand once,
even to scratch,
since we've been here,

which seems like hours
even though it's probably only been
twenty minutes.

I don't know how
they're going to manage it
when the food comes.

Dylan and I are just sitting here
across from them in the booth,
trying to make small talk.

Our thighs
aren't even touching
on the seat.

At the Movies

I'm sitting between Henry and Dylan.
Dylan's holding my hand,
but I can tell he isn't *feeling* it.

He's actually watching the movie.
I mean *really* watching it,
like it doesn't even matter that I'm here.

And the saddest part is
that I don't care.
I'd almost rather snuggle up to Henry.

But he's too busy holding hands
(and everything else)
with Grace.

WALKING HOME

The light changes
and Dylan and I head across the street,
arm in arm.

That's when it happens:
I notice our reflection in
the window of Starbucks
and I get this weird feeling
that something isn't quite right.
Only I can't put my finger on it.

Then it hits me:
what's wrong is that it looks like
I'm *taller* than Dylan,
which is totally bizarre
because I'm wearing my flattest shoes
and I know for a fact
that he's taller than me.

At least he *was* taller
six weeks ago
when we first started
going out together.

I've heard of people
outgrowing relationships,
but *this* is ridiculous.

Good Night

We're standing under the porch light,
face to face,
leaning our foreheads together.

He's playing with my fingers,
whispering something
about what a great time he had tonight.

And all I can think about
is that his hands look smaller than mine,
like the hands of a little boy.

Q and A with Chaz

"Do you have a boyfriend?"
"Yes."

"Do you have a girlfriend?"
"Yes."

"Who is she?"
"You."

Me?!

"Yikes."
"Yeah."

HIM

I wake up
thinking about him.

All day long
I'm dreaming about him.

I fall asleep
thinking about him.

Only
it's the *wrong* him.

If It Weren't for Dylan

I wouldn't be feeling
like a
low-down
dirty rotten
good-for-nothing
deceitful
despicable snake.

I could just be
enjoying this thing with Chaz
totally and completely,
without one
single
speck
of guilt,

if it weren't for Dylan.

It's Strange

I used to wish like anything
that he'd want to spend
every
minute with me.

But now that he's practically
glued himself to my side,
I keep tripping over him.
Like he's my Siamese twin or something.

He's always
pushing me
to go further
but I just don't want to

and maybe it's because
I'm not ready
or maybe it's because
I don't love him enough.

Or maybe
I don't
love him
at all.

Or maybe I never did.

Too Late

Way back in the beginning of September,
when I wasn't even sure yet
if he liked me,
I used to imagine what I'd do
if Dylan told me he loved me.

In my fantasy I'd just throw back my head
with a triumphant sexy laugh,
and then
he'd rake his fingers through my hair
and kiss me hard on the mouth.

But tonight
when he finally said the magic words,
I didn't laugh and he didn't kiss me.
He just peered at me with this worried look
and I suddenly felt like crying.

And Right Then, Murphy Popped into My Head

It was so weird, but he did.
And I found myself wondering
if anyone has ever told Murphy
that they love him.

His mother maybe has.
Or his father.
But I wondered
if a girl ever has.

Or if one ever will.
And somehow
that made me feel even sadder
than I already was.

And then I found myself wondering
if this was the one time,
the first and last time,
that a boy would ever say it to *me*.

TONIGHT'S CHAZ CHAT

He writes:
"Of course,
I don't really care what you look like,
But—
what do you look like?"

I think for a second
before I answer:
"Well, people say
I'm sort of a combination of
Marilyn Monroe, Julia Roberts,
and Madonna.
What do you look like?"

And he writes back:
"Same."

I burst out laughing
and suddenly find myself imagining
what his laugh sounds like,
and what his lips look like,
and how they'd feel
covering mine.

LITTERBOX ICG

If I could marry a font
I'd marry his.

I just love it,
the way all of the letters *lean*
at those quirky little angles.

They remind me of the letters
in those thought balloons
in the Sunday funnies,
like words that Snoopy
or Garfield
might be thinking.

And those question marks are—
well, they're adorable.
They just *are* somehow.

If I could marry a font,
I would definitely marry his.

SHOWER

I step into the steam
and let the water
rinse my body clean
while rivers flow in ribbons
down my arms
and waterfalls caress my breasts
and swirl in lazy trickles
to my thighs
as soap melts into creamy suds
that slide across my skin
like foaming clouds,

and all the while
I'm thinking about Chaz,
imagining he's with me in this mist,
imagining he's
with me . . .

BIT BY BIT

"Okay," I write.
"Describe how you've been picturing me."
"I don't have to picture you," he replies.
"I've got a very powerful computer."

For a second I panic,
thinking of all the times
I've chatted with him
wearing my ratty old nightgown.

But then he writes, "Just kidding."
And I write, "Whew!"
And he writes,
"Actually, I see you as a curly-haired redhead
with sea green eyes, very wise,
and a few freckles
sprinkled across your perfect nose."

"Right!" I reply,
"Except for the hair, the eyes,
and that part about the freckles and the nose."

Then I add,
"What do you look like?"
"Why don't we meet
so you can find out?" he asks.

"Gulp," I answer.
"Ditto," he writes.

I Don't Know How to Tell Dylan

I used
to think I was
in love
with him.

But that
must have been
a different him.
Or maybe a different me.

Because
when I look at him now
I see a friend,
not a boyfriend.

And when he kisses me,
all I feel is
the overwhelming
overness of it.

When Dylan Cried

When Dylan cried,
I felt way more powerful
than I wanted to feel.

I started crying too.
I couldn't help it.

And then we hugged each other
tighter than we ever had before,
knowing that we never would again.

LOWER THAN LOW

He said he wasn't mad.
He said he understood.
He said he'd be okay.

So,
why do I feel this way?

WE SAID WE'D STILL BE FRIENDS, BUT

Whenever Dylan sees me
he pretends he doesn't notice
and he tosses both his arms
around the nearest pretty girl.

Whenever I see Dylan
I kneel down to tie my shoelace
or start searching through my backpack
like I've lost my favorite pen.

When we *can't* avoid each other
Dylan acts so glad to see me—
only now he calls me Sophie.
I'm not Sapphire anymore.

DELETED

Tonight Chaz asked me:
"What's your favorite thing to do?"
I wasn't sure what to say
so I just wrote back:
"I don't know. What's yours?"

He's not real quick at typing,
but I had to wait even longer than usual
for his answer to pop onto my screen:
"I like to jerk off in libraries."

The words just sat there staring at me,
like something ugly
scratched on a restroom wall.
I felt as if I'd been punched
hard
in the stomach.
I couldn't breathe.

"You're kidding, right?"
I typed back.
"No. I'm not," he wrote.

I read those words again and again,
trying to get myself to believe them.
I felt like I was
plummeting through cyberspace
out of control,
until I took some deep breaths,
pulled myself together
and wrote:
"Consider yourself permanently deleted."
Then, I clicked off.

And just now,
I changed my e-mail address.

Chat Room Chump

How could I ever have let
such a pervert into my life like that?
*"Come right in, Mr. Disgusting,
make yourself at home."*
I could have ended up as a headline:
STUPID TEEN MURDERED BY CYBER PSYCHO!

And to think
that just last night
we were talking about maybe even
trying to meet each other
"in the flesh,"
as he put it.

What if
we'd actually arranged that meeting?
What if
he'd chosen the library as the place?
What if
when I got there he'd been—

WHEN I TELL THEM

Grace shivers
and pretends to gag.

Rachel's eyes
quadruple in size.

Then they scoop me up
in a three-way hug,

and whisk me off
to the movies.

Their treat.

THE HALLOWEEN DANCE IS COMING UP

Rachel says
she'd rather go trick or treating.
Grace says me too.
I say me three.

But Rachel says
if we don't go
it'll probably turn out to be
the best dance of the millennium.

And Grace says
besides, trick or treating's too risky.
What if someone saw us?
We'd never live it down.

I say
I just wish I knew where Chaz lived
so I could go over there
and throw rotten eggs at his computer.

Shopping for a Dress to Wear to the Dance

Scene One: At the Sale Rack

"How about this one, Soso?" my mother says,
holding up a dress with these
enormous pink roses plastered all over it.

"Mom, I do *not* want to go to the dance
dressed as a potted plant."
"Of course not.
I was thinking of a rosebush."

"A rosebush?!"
"You'll see what I mean when you try it on.
It'll look so darling *on*."

"But, Mom. It's ugly."
"How can you tell
if you don't try it on?"

"Mom, I hate everything about it.
I like this little black one.
I could go as a beatnik in this one."

"But being a rosebush would be so original,
so creative . . ."
"So kindergarten!"

"Then try them both on.
But you're gonna love the flowered one.
You'll see."

Scene Two: In the Dressing Room

"What *do* you think?" I say,
twirling in front of the three-way mirror
in the gorgeous black dress.

"Perfect. For a funeral.
Besides. It's too tight.
Now, take that one off
and try on the beautiful one."

Scene Three:
In the Dressing Room, Moments Later

116

"It looks even more hideous *on*, Mom."
"I think it flatters your figure."
"I don't care what you think."

"That's right.
Why *should* you care?
I'm only your mother."

"Aw, Mom.
Please.
Don't cry."

Scene Four: At the Cash Register

No dialogue.
Only the crinkly sound
of the flowered dress
being slipped into a paper bag.

Okay, Here's The Plan:

I'll call the store from a phone booth
and ask them to hold the black dress
for two weeks.

I'll baby-sit
for the Weingartens
and the Bigelows
and the Devlins.

And I'll give up lunches,
which will save me
another couple of dollars a day
right there.

Then, when I have enough,
I'll sneak over,
buy the dress
and stash it at Rachel's.

On the night of the dance,
I'll leave the house
in the rose disaster dress
but do a quick change at Rachel's.

And what my mother
doesn't know,
won't hurt me.

THE MINUTE MR. SCHULTZ LEAVES THE ROOM

Art class degenerates
into a giggling gabfest
about Halloween Dance costumes.

The only one still working is Murphy,
hunched over his desk,
painting a gray road,

a road
that's fading away
into the gray emptiness of the horizon

and in the foreground, just
one
tree,

a tree that looks like a poem,
a tree that makes me feel
like weeping.

2 WEEKS, 6 DIAPERS, 5 PUPPET SHOWS, AND 9 READINGS OF "GOODNIGHT MOON" LATER

Rachel donates half of her tuna sandwich.

Grace parts with her pickle.

Henry gives me his carrot sticks.

Zak offers what's left of his chips.

Danny hands over

the remains of his beef jerky.

And when I stuff today's lunch money

into the jar,

there's finally enough

in the Gorgeous Black Dress Fund

to actually buy

the gorgeous black dress.

THE MOCKINGBIRD

I'm watching him up there,
silhouetted on the wire,
alone against
the silky blue sky,
belting out the songs
that he's borrowed
from all the other birds,

trying on
one voice after another,
pausing briefly
between each one
to see if he's attracting
the girl bird
of his dreams,

and every now and then
he dances up into the air,
fluttering in a loop
that shows off the patches of white
etched on his wings,
before landing back down on the wire
to begin another song.

And as I watch him,
I'm feeling a lot like him,
like a feathery creature
balancing on a wire,
trying on lots of different voices
to see which one
works best

and every now and then,
doing a little twirl
out on the dance floor,
hoping the boy bird of my dreams
will fly by and notice me,
flutter down beside me
and ask me to dance.

Three Hours Before the Dance

Even though I wash it,
twice,
with shampoo that's especially formulated
with essential fatty acids
derived from natural botanic oils
to replace valuable lipids
and restore the emollients necessary
for the hair to remain
soft, pliable and supple
with a healthy, radiant shine,

and even though I remove
the excess moisture from my hair
and evenly distribute a small amount
of instant reconstructor and detangler
to enhance strength and manageability,

and even though
I work it through to the ends,
leaving it on for three minutes
and then rinse thoroughly before adding
the revolutionary polymerized
electrolytic moisture potion
that actually repairs split ends
while providing flexible styling control
by infusing the roots with twenty-three
essential pro-vitamins,

and even though I massage it in
to make my hair feel instantly softer
and fuller with added shaping power,
and then rinse it again
with lukewarm water,
towel dry and apply the desired amount
of styling gel to the palm of my hand,
and then comb it through
and blow it dry,

it still looks pathetic.

Two Hours Before the Dance

Eyeliner
should be a no-brainer
for someone as good at drawing
as I am.

But even though
I'm extra careful,
the line on the left eyelid
ends up just a tad thinner
than the line on the right eyelid.

And when I try
to even them out,
the left line ends up
thicker than the right line.

And forty minutes later,
when I finally manage to get them even,
they're both half an inch wide—
which is *not* a good look,
even for a beatnik.

So I scrub it all off
and settle instead
for some "Just Say Yes"
Moisture Lick Luminous Lip Gel.

In *my* case, less is definitely more.

One Hour Before the Dance

We pull up in front of Rachel's house.
Mom kisses me on the cheek,
says I look dope in my new dress
(she's trying to sound so *with* it
but she's so totally *without* it)
and tells me to have a good time.
Like she really *means* it.

And for once
she doesn't give me the evil eye
and warn me to watch out for the boys.

Maybe she's using reverse psychology.
Maybe she's finally growing up.
Maybe she's just *giving* up.
Or maybe
she's terrified
that I'll never get married
and end up living with her and dad forever.

Now
there's
a scary thought.

She Has No Idea

That I'm about to go in there
and switch into the gorgeous black dress.

Do I feel guilty?
Sort of.
But not enough to keep me from doing it.

A girl's got to do
what a girl's got to do.

R AND G ANSWER THE DOOR

Rachel takes one look at the
gigantic pink roses all over my dress
and says, "Oh, Fifi. You poor thing.
No wonder you were so obsessed."

Grace says, "Are you thirsty?
I could go and get the hose . . ."
I say, "Thanks. But I'd rather have
a swig of some Miracle-Gro."

We burst out laughing,
race up the stairs
and lock ourselves in Rachel's room
to perform the Sacred Transformations.

Grace slips into her Juliet costume
(Henry's going as Romeo).
Rachel puts on her Bert costume
(Danny's going as Ernie).

And me?
I'm just going as
the beatnik who's deliriously happy
not to be going as a rosebush.

I Slip into the Gorgeous Black Dress

And instantly feel
as smooth and as soft and as silky
as the satin that it's made of.

I feel as slinky as a model in this dress.
So full of possibilities.
Like *anything* could happen.

And something *is*
going to happen.
Tonight.

I can feel it coming.
And I'll be wearing this dress
when it *does*.

Sometimes I just *know* things.

At the Dance

Mr. Schultz is
selling tickets at the door,
dressed as Howard Stern.

Not a pretty picture.

The gym's been transformed
into a haunted house,
which basically means that some spider webs
are hanging from the basketball hoops.

It's loud,
dark,
crowded,
sweaty,

and I'm *very* glad to be here.

GUESS WHO?

I'm dancing with a bunch of girls,
bouncing like kernels of popcorn
in a hot frying pan,

when this guy pushes through the crowd
and starts dancing right in front of me.
Real close.

He's wearing this evil-looking mask,
and I don't recognize his eyes.
He seems older than the other boys . . .

And I suddenly think:
What if this is Chaz?
What if he's tracked me down somehow?

I
stop
breathing.

Then Rachel shoves him
and says,
"Move over, Fletcher."

And my lungs
fill back up
with air.

Is It My Imagination

Or is the drummer
staring right at
me?

His wild eyes
are dancing with mine,
swimming into mine.

He's choosing *me* to play to, *me*
out of all the other girls
at this dance.

I'm
afraid
to blink.

But the second the song ends,
this blonde leaps out
from behind the velvet curtains

and kisses him
so hard on the mouth
that it looks like it hurts.

After that
he doesn't look my way
again.

THERE'S DYLAN

Dressed in those pale blue hospital scrubs
that they wear on *ER*,
with a stethoscope dangling around his neck
and his hair all grown in and spiked up,
wailing on an air guitar.

Looking *so* hot.

I've got this crazy urge
to run up and tell him
I'm feeling faint,
like maybe I'm having
a heart attack or something.

(Well, I *am*, sort of.)

And then
I could keel over
and he'd have to catch me in his arms
and give me some emergency
mouth-to-mouth resuscitation.

I could use some of that right about now—

But here comes Angela Pierson,
sneaking up behind him,
putting her
delicate little hands
over his eyes.

Dressed like a nurse.

MASKED MAN

He walks up to me
and holds out his arms.
I ease into them
and we begin to dance.

The music
is slow
and
saxophony.

I can feel the heat
of his hands penetrating
the thin fabric of my dress
at the small of my back.

His fingers roam up to my shoulders,
melting away my shyness,
as he draws me close enough
to feel my breasts against his chest.

We move together,
breathe together,
my hands gripping his shoulders,
his thigh pressed between mine.

I don't have a clue who I'm dancing with,
but our bodies are acting like old friends,
as though *they* know something
we don't know.

WHAT I WANT

I want
to keep on dancing
slow with him.

I want
to keep on dancing
on and on.

I want
to dance real slow till dawn
like this.

I want
to dance and dance
and dance,

then kiss.

THE SONG ENDS

But I float
in my masked man's arms
for a few seconds more,

and when I lean back to look into his eyes,
they're so alive,
so totally locked to mine,

that when he takes my hand
and presses it to his heart,
I feel like my knees might give way.

Then Whoever He Is
bows deeply,
and disappears into the crowd.

(I *knew* something
was going to happen
tonight.)

Wherefore Art Thou?

When I snap out of it,
I start scouring the gym for him,
kicking myself for not even thinking
of asking him his name,
for not just reaching up
and whipping off his mask
to catch a glimpse of his face
while I still had the chance.

But no matter how hard I search,
I can't find him anywhere,
and when the last note of the last song
fades away,
I drift outside
to wait for my mother,
wondering if there could be such a thing
as "love at first dance."

I'd Pictured It Before

Where it would happen.
Whose hand it would be.
How it would feel.
But never like this.

Never waiting on the corner
for my mother to pick me up
after a school dance,
the last of my girlfriends already gone,
standing next to
a couple of tenth-grade boys
I've seen around school.
Them joking with each other, guzzling beer,
me wishing my mother wasn't always so late.

I never thought
it would happen *this* way—
with the guy standing closest to me
suddenly bursting out laughing
and grabbing my breasts
with his slimy paws,
squeezing them for a split second
that seems to last forever.

I never once envisioned
the devirginization of my breasts
happening like this,
with the guy and his scumbag buddy
slapping five afterwards
as though he's just done something
to be proud of,
the two of them snickering
and nudging each other,
the one who did it whispering,
"I told you they were real.
You owe me five bucks."

I never imagined myself
just standing there
with this huge lump in my throat,
feeling so mad
that steam would practically be
blasting out of my ears.

I never pictured my hand
morphing into a fist
or the fist swinging out
to sock his jaw.
I never knew how great it would feel
to slam my knuckles into his chin,
how satisfying it would be
to smash my foot into his friend's knee,
how good it would be to watch them
backing away from me wide-eyed,
stumbling before they turned and ran.

And I never ever expected
that when my mother pulled up
a second later
and I leapt into the car,
that I'd be feeling like
slapping five with her

and shouting out "Yes!"

How Could I Have Forgotten?

My mother
whips around,
slashing me
with the knives
gleaming in her eyes,
and whispers in dark
soap opera tones,

"That dress!"

TEARS

Usually
I can feel them coming,
feel them swirling in my chest
like a swarm of angry bees,

buzzing up through my neck
and filling my head,
till it feels like a balloon
getting ready to burst.

Usually
there's time to at least *try* to stop them
before they sting out through my eyes
and slip down my cheeks like hot wax.

But not this time.

After the Fight with Mom

It's lying there
where she threw it
after she tore it apart,

while the echo
of the rrrrrriiiippping
still ricocheted off my bedroom walls,

right where it landed
after she yanked it off the hanger
and wrenched it into two ragged shards,

after the toads
stopped springing
from her lips,

after her red-rimmed eyes
stopped trying to escape
from their sockets.

It's lying there where she threw it,
in a heap,
like roadkill:

my no-longer-gorgeous black dress.

All I Want to Know Is

How come just a minute ago,
when my mother was talking to me,
she made her voice
so dead and flat and hollow
that the mere sound of it
flooded me with guilt,

but when the telephone rang
just now,
and she picked it up,
her voice was a perfectly cheerful,
bright and lively
chirp?

And how come
this makes me feel
like slapping her so hard
across her face
that the shape of my hand
will leave a stinging print?

I HATE HER

I hate her for destroying my dress.
Hate her for going ballistic.
Hate her for all her screaming and crying
and for making me feel
like I'm the worst daughter
in the world.

I hate her for being so controlling.
Hate her for being so melodramatic.
Hate her for fighting with Dad all the time
and for never once admitting
in her whole entire life
that anything could *ever*
possibly be *her* fault.

I hate her for watching TV all day.
Hate her for not ever talking to me.
Hate her for not ever listening to me.
And I hate her for not being more
like Rachel's mom.
Or like Grace's.

I hate her.
I hate her.
I *hate* her.

But I hate hating her.
I hate it.

I'd Rather Be Grounded

My mother's down there in the basement
right now,
where she always goes
when she gets like this.

Down there in her bathrobe,
in the clammy dark,
sprawled on the old mattress,
stuffing Hershey's Kisses into her mouth,
chain-smoking, watching her soaps,
and weeping.

Weeping just loud enough
to make me wish I was deaf,
just loud enough
to make me wish I had the courage
to storm down there
and yank her back upstairs.

My mother's down there
right now,
and she hasn't been up for days
except to cook our meals,
dragging herself around the kitchen
like a zombie,
tossing the food onto the plates,
tossing the plates onto the table,

then trudging back down into her hole
without saying a word.

At least Dad's managed to get home
in time for dinner these past three nights,
like he doesn't want me
to have to go through it alone.

But I haven't been able
to swallow a bite,
even so.

Maybe if I hadn't
gone behind her back to buy that dress,
maybe if I hadn't
forgotten to change out of it
before she picked me up,
maybe if I hadn't
lied to her in the first place,
my mother wouldn't be down there
in the basement

right now.

My Masked Man Would Know

I bet I wouldn't even
have to tell him
about my mother.

He'd just look into my eyes
and know how it feels
to be buried under an avalanche of guilt.

Know
that I needed to be held.
Know that I needed to be kissed.

So he'd hold me and kiss me,
and for awhile
I wouldn't care *where* my mother was.

SHE'S BACK

Maybe it was the note
I slipped under the door to the cellar.
The one in which I apologized abjectly
for sneaking around behind her back
and said I missed her
and couldn't stand having her
living in the basement
for one more second.

Or maybe she just got tired
of being miserable.

But when I got home from school today,
she was actually out front in the yard
raking up some leaves.
She even smiled at me.
And for a second it almost looked like
she was going to say she was sorry
for guilting me into buying that ugly dress
in the first place.

She *didn't* say it.
But the smile was *good*.

Eleven P.M.

There's this
real corny thing
that Channel 5 does every night
after the late movie,
just before the news comes on.

They flash this sign on the screen
that says:
"It's eleven p.m.
Do you know where
your children are?"

And just now,
when it came on,
I heard this little tap tap tap on the wall
coming from my mother's bedroom,
and I tapped right back.

FOREARMS

Okay.
So I've become obsessed with arms.
Well, *forearms*, actually.
His forearms.

I'm painfully aware
of just how bizarre this is
but *ever* since the dance,
I can't seem to get a grip.

Forearms Я me.
Today in the cafeteria
Grace said, "There goes Tommy A.
Look at those buns."

But I was thinking,
"Look at those forearms.
I wonder if they
belong to my masked man."

Wherever I go, I'm checking out forearms.
I'm thinking, "How would *those* feel
wrapped around me? Or those?
Are *those* my masked man's forearms?"

I've got to find him.
Him and those forearms of his,

the ones that devastated me
when he held me in them

just ten days,
fourteen hours,
thirty-two minutes
and twenty-nine seconds ago.

Okay.
So I don't
really know
how many seconds.

WHEN I'M NOT OGLING FOREARMS

I'm making my way
through the halls at school,
searching every boy's face
for my masked man's eyes,

but it's harder than finding Waldo
because the truth is
I can't even remember
what color they were.

I guess it wasn't how they *looked*
that got to me.
It was how it *felt*
when they connected to mine—

like this door
was opening up inside of me
that had never been opened before,
and his soul was walking right in.

THE PERSONALS

I wish I could put an ad
in the school paper:

WANTED DESPERATELY—the boy who owns the
arms and eyes that held me at the Halloween dance.
Haven't been able to think about anything else since
that night. Haven't been able to breathe. Call 555-
9910 before I shrivel up and die!

GRACE DOESN'T GET IT

She says she can't figure out
why I'm getting so worked up
about a guy I've never even said
two words to.

So I remind her
how worked up she got about Henry
before she'd ever said
two words to *him*.

"That was different," she says.
"Henry wasn't wearing a mask."

But Rachel
totally gets it.

"Fee's in love with him even though
she hasn't seen his face," she says.
"Don't you see how incredibly deep that is?
She's in love with his *essence*."

"She's not in love with his essence,"
Grace says.
"She's in love with his body parts."
"That's *so* not true," I say.
"I'm in love with
the *essence* of his body parts."

And we all crack up.

Twenty Questions

1. Is he as obsessed with me,
   as I am with him?
2. Is he thinking about me
   at this very moment?
3. Has he *ever* thought about me?
4. Has he never thought about me?
5. Was our dance as amazing for him
   as it was for me?
6. Will I always feel this way?
7. Am I going to spend the rest of my life
   fixating on him?
8. How much sense does that make?
9. Why can't I stop thinking about him?
10. Am I totally losing it?
11. Do I know him?
12. Is he a freshman?
13. Does he even go to my school?
14. Why hasn't he revealed himself to me?
15. Will he *ever* reveal himself to me?
16. What's he waiting for?
17. Does he already have a girlfriend?
18. Does he think I'm ugly?
19. Does he think I'm an idiot?
20. *Am* I an idiot?

Gray Sky Blues

It's been overcast
for more than
a week now.

Heavy clouds hang low
like a thick gray soup
boiling overhead.

I'm gray
through and through.
Even my thoughts are gray.

If I cut my finger
I'd bleed
gray blood.

No sign of sun.
No sign of blue sky.
No sign of masked man.

It's going to be a long gray winter.

At the Beach

Rachel's mother
(who I wish was *my* mother)
has driven us down to the Cape
to let us get our yaya's out, she said.
Whatever.

Even though it's still overcast,
there are all these
slivers of sunlight
reaching down through the clouds
like *God's* fingers,

looking like if one of them
were to touch me right now
something magical,
something masked-mannish
might even happen.

But the mystic rays
are shining down onto the sea
instead of me,
probably making some lucky
halibut's day.

I Bet He's a Jerk Anyway

One of those real hunky, gorgeous,
rich, stuck-up jerks
who thinks he's the greatest thing since
the invention of the cell phone.

It wouldn't surprise me one bit
if it even turned out to be
Hamilton Hurley III.
Or that annoyingly perfect Peter Scrinshaw.

I mean
he *must* be a jerk.
Because if he wasn't,
he wouldn't be torturing me like this.

I Can't Believe What Just Happened

Zak asked me out.

On a *date*.

Zak
who I used to call Wacky Zakky
in preschool.

We've been friends since
before we even knew the difference
between boys and girls.

I'm still not sure *he* does.

I hope I didn't embarrass him
when I laughed.
It's just that I thought he was kidding.

God.

Zak.

Why did you have to ask me out?
Why did I have to say yes?
I can't believe I said yes.

I can't wait until tomorrow night is over.

Tomorrow Night Is Over

We went out for pizza
and then we went bowling.
That part wasn't too bad.
But when we were walking home
and he tried to hold my hand,
I freaked.

It wasn't like I was afraid
he was going to confess
to being my masked man or anything.
There was less than zero chance of that.
But I had no idea how to break it to him
that I wasn't interested.

Then I got this sudden
flash of inspiration
and told him that
I couldn't possibly hold hands with him
because I thought of him as my brother,
as the brother I'd never had,

and I didn't want to give up my brother
just to have a boyfriend
because I'll probably have
lots of boyfriends in my life
but only one brother
and I wanted that brother to be him.

Then I gave him this real sisterly hug.
He looked confused but kind of flattered.
And I was so relieved that I'd
thought of a way to reject him
without actually making him feel rejected,
that I could have kissed him.

But I figured I better not.
Under the circumstances.

THANKSGIVING

I'm thankful
that I'm actually starting to forget
how amazing it felt to dance with him.
I'm thankful that when I try to remember
that steamy look he had in his eyes,
I can barely picture it.

I'm thankful
to finally be able
to lie in bed at night
and occasionally see something *other*
than that mask of his
floating in front of my face.

I'm thankful
to be able to have
three or four thoughts
in a row
that are not even *about* him.
(It's that fifth one that's the killer.)

I'm thankful
that I've almost managed
to convince myself
that I'm not
obsessed with him
anymore.

Gelt Shmelt

Hanukkah's here early this year.
Whoop-de-do.

Why can't it just stay put on the calendar?
Like Christmas does.
Christmas is so reliable.

Sure, Hanukkah's got its good points.
Like that it lasts for eight days.
But it was much more fun when I was little.

Back when my parents used to give me presents.
Things that they actually shopped for
and took the time to wrap up.

Now they just hand me a check
(when they finish arguing
about what the amount should be).

This year
they haven't even bothered
lighting the menorah.

And Mom said
she didn't feel up to making her latkes.

I sure miss them.

Winter Break

Every single person
in the city of Cambridge, Massachusetts,
has skipped town.
Every single person but me.

Rachel's family went to Bermuda.
Grace's went to Florida.
My family never goes
anywhere.

Not to Bermuda.
Not to Florida.
Not to Jamaica.
Not even to frigging Vermont.

My parents say they can't afford vacations
and putting me through college
(which is about the only thing
I've ever heard them agree on).

I say
I can't wait till college.
At least *then*
I'll be *going* somewhere.

THE WEIRDEST THING HAPPENED TONIGHT

I was looking out my window,
watching the swirling flakes
of the first snowfall
hushing the whole world,
when this white dove
fluttered down onto my balcony railing.

I stood very still, staring at it.
It stared right back at me
with this bright glass eye,
then began cooing softly,
like it was trying to tell me
that everything would be all right.

I felt like we were drifting together
in the same mirage
until it flew away.
And now that it's gone,
I'm wondering if it
was ever really there.

I Dreamt About That White Dove Last Night

We were flying together
over the streets of Boston.
I had these strong white wings
that knew just what to do.

And when I woke up just now,
I started thinking about how
lots of people come to Boston
on vacation all the time.

So I decided to pretend
I'm one of *them* today,
and take *myself* on a vacation.
Only I won't have to leave town to do it.

Who needs parents, anyway?

Bon Voyage

Mom looks up from the TV
as I head towards the front door.
"Where are you off to?" she asks.

When I tell her my vacation plan,
she raises an eyebrow.
"Clever," she says with a little smile.

And for a second it seems like
she might even be thinking about asking
if she can come along.

I sort of really wish she would,
but I sort of really wish
she wouldn't.

It's a moot point
anyhow,
because all she says is,

"Well,
make sure you're home before dark.
There are lots of weirdos out there."

Then
she goes back to watching
From Martha's Kitchen.

First Stop: Breakfast at the Ritz-Carlton Hotel

The waiter's nostrils flare
when all I order is
a cup of Earl Grey
and one measly scone.

I pull out my sketchbook
and draw the scone before I eat it,
plus the hundred-year-old lady
with the huge hat
at the table by the window.

I sip my tea
while eavesdropping on two women
discussing the relative merits
of their male masseuses,

and try to imagine
what it would be like
to be lying naked underneath a sheet
while a strange man rubbed oil
all over my body.

Then the waiter brings the check
on a fancy little silver tray
and scowls at me while I sketch it,
before I pay it.

SECOND STOP: SHOPPING IN FILENE'S BARGAIN BASEMENT WITHOUT MY MOTHER

I just found
the most outrageous lime green panties
with these little squiggly things
that look just like sperm
swimming all over them.

I picked them out.
By myself.
And no one tried to talk me out of them.
No one pressured me to choose
the darling frilly pink ones instead.

I'm going to walk right over
to that cash register and
buy five pairs of these sperm panties.
And I'm going to cherish them.
Always.

THIRD STOP: A VISIT TO THE MUSEUM OF FINE ARTS

I head straight upstairs
to the Impressionist Gallery,
to see my favorite painting:
Le Bal à Bougival.

I sit down
on the oak bench,
gaze up at
the life-sized dancing couple

and let myself slip
through the gilded frame,
right into Renoir's
so soft world . . .

I want to be that woman
in the long white dress,
waltzing in the arms
of that redheaded man.

I want to feel the heat
of his hand holding mine,
and press my cheek
to the fur of his beard.

I want to feel the thrill
of his arm round my waist,
his eyes on my face,
his leg between mine.

I want to be that woman
in *Le Bal à Bougival*
and dance forever
with that unmasked man . . .

But Suddenly—

"Sophie."
Someone is saying my name.
"Sophie?"
Asking it,
like a question.
And I'm wrenched from the painting
and snapped back to the reality
of the hard oak bench.

There's someone sitting next to me.
Speaking to me.
"How ya doin?"
It's . . . Murphy.
MURPHY?!
And he looks
so happy to see me
his tail's practically wagging.

"Oh! Hi," I say,
trying to sound friendly, but wishing
I could get the heck out of here.
"It's an awesome painting,
isn't it?" he says.
"Yeah," I say.
"My all-time favorite," he says.
"Mine, too," I admit.

MURPHY TELLS ME

That he has a book about Renoir
and that it says in there
that the dancing man
is Renoir's friend, Paul Lhote.

He tells me
that the woman is
a seventeen-year-old girl
named Marie-Clementine Valadon.

He says
when she was older
Marie-Clementine became
a well-known painter herself.

And Murphy says
there's something about her
that reminds him
of me.

WHAT HAVE I DONE?

Oh, no.
Tell me
that I didn't do
what I think I just did.

I didn't
ask Murphy
to have lunch with me just now,
did I?

Man oh Manischevitz.
Lunch with Murphy.
In a public place.
This is going to be totally *Twilight Zone*.

FOURTH STOP: LUNCH AT PIZZERIA REGINA WITH MURPHY

We climb the stairs,
and duck out of the cold
into the roasted garlic sweet tomato scent
of Regina's.

I slide into the ancient wooden booth,
positioning myself with my back to the door,
so if anyone I know walks in,
they won't see me sitting with Murphy.

"What *do* you want on the pizza,
Marie-Clementine?" he asks.
I can't help smiling at this.
"Whatever *vous* want," I say.

And when Murphy smiles back at me,
I realize
that I've never seen
him smile before.

And it's nice, his smile.

WHILE WAITING FOR PIZZA

Murphy reaches into his backpack
and pulls out a sketchbook
and a pencil.

He says the light
coming in through the window
is perfect right now.

So I reach into *my* backpack
and pull out *my* sketchbook and pencil.
"It *is* perfect, isn't it?" I say.

Then we grin at each other
and start sketching everything
in sight.

Fifth Stop: Skating on the Frog Pond on Boston Common

We pull on the rented skates,
wobble our way to the edge of the pond,
and glide out onto the ice,
weaving ourselves into the flow
of the darting mob.

Almost instantly,
this kid going way past the speed limit,
smacks into me.
Murphy has to grab my hand
to keep me from falling.

He lets go of it a second later,
after he steadies me.
And what's truly bizarre
is that I almost feel disappointed
when he does.

"I know a better place to skate,"
Murphy says. "It's kind of a secret spot.
No one to knock you over but me.
I'll take you there tomorrow
if you want."

Was that *me* who just said
"I'd like that"?

Before We Say Goodbye

Murphy writes something down
on a scrap of paper from his sketchbook
and presses it into my hand.

It's something scary.
Something numerical.
Something distinctly phone numberish.

"So you can call me
about going skating tomorrow,"
he says.

It's such a little slip of paper.
It would be so easy to lose it.
I wouldn't have to call him,

if I lost it.

E-MAIL FROM RACHEL AND GRACE

The one from Rachel says
that her hotel has a pool
with a waterfall in it,
and that the lifeguard is devastating
(she's already drowned twice),
and that her bungalow is painted
a color called "sky blue pink,"
and that she feels guilty because
she doesn't miss Danny one bit,
and that she's getting an extreme tan.

The one from Grace says
that she was walking on the beach
in Boca Raton with her cousin
and they met this old man named Harold
who has just about
the most amazing garden ever,
which he grew completely
out of mystery seeds
that washed up on the beach,
and that she misses
the bejesus out of Henry,
and that she's getting an extreme tan.

They both say they miss me
and want to know
what I'm doing to keep busy.
So I'm going to e them back
and tell them all about
the vacation I took myself on today.

Well,
maybe not all . . .

Okay

So maybe my old fantasy
about kissing Murphy
did flit across my mind
once or twice today.

But it wasn't like a
physical attraction kind of thing.
It was more like an
I-feel-sorry-for-him kind of thing.

Because probably no one
has *ever* kissed him before.
And maybe no one ever *will* kiss him
his whole life long.

Unless I *do*.
And it *would* be sort of neat
to be the very first girl
that a guy ever kissed.

But just because I thought about it
doesn't mean I'd ever really *do* it.
Since if I did, he'd probably think
I wanted to be his girlfriend or something.

Which I definitely *don't*.

HE TOOK ME THERE THIS AFTERNOON

To this hidden pond
in a little clearing
deep in the woods near the reservoir.

We decided
we'd call it
Valadon Pond.

Now I'm soaking in the tub,
trying to thaw myself out,
watching the steam curl into question marks,

remembering the feel of
the shivery wind
rosing my cheeks,

the soft scents
of pine needle
and new snow,

the mirror-smooth ice
gliding past
beneath my skates

and the warmth
of his gloved hand
holding mine.

Oh, Man

I probably
shouldn't have let him
hold my hand.

What if it
gave him
the wrong idea?

I hope
he doesn't think
that I like him now.

I mean
I *do* like him,
but I don't *like* him.

And Speaking of Regrets

I didn't mind so much
when he gave me *his* phone number.
But why did I have to give him
mine?

When he asked me for it,
I could have just said that my mother
doesn't let me get phone calls from boys,
even if they're only *friends,* like *he* is.

That would have made it
perfectly clear to him
exactly where I stand
romance-wise.

But I didn't.
I just gave it to him.
Like an idiot.
And now I freak out

every time the phone rings.

HE DIDN'T CALL LAST NIGHT

And he didn't call this morning.
Poor guy.
He's probably trying
to work up his courage.

Anyway,
I didn't want to
just hang around the house
watching my mother watch TV,

so after lunch
I came over here
to Pearl's Art Supplies
to spend some of my Hanukkah gelt.

I just bought one of those
real serious sketchbooks
with the black leather cover
that I've always wanted.

And some
professional drawing pencils,
with this super-soft lead,
that I've been lusting after.

I bought a few for Murphy, too.
For Christmas.
From a friend to a friend.
Purely platonic.

He'll understand.

Won't he?

MURPHY FINALLY CALLS

My mother answers the phone.
Her eyes narrow.
But she hands it over to me
and I take it into my bedroom
for some privacy.

That's when Murphy asks me
if I want to go out
to the movies with him tonight.

There's something about
the way he phrases this,
I think it's the "tonight" part,
that worries me.

So I say,
"You mean *go out* out?
Like on an actual date?"

He's silent for a second.
And then he says,
"Well, yeah. I guess."

For a minute
I think about using the
"brother I never had" routine on him.

But it doesn't feel right.

So I take a deep
I-don't-want-to-hurt-him-
but-I-have-to-tell-him breath
and then I say that I think
he's an amazingly cool
and fun to be with guy,
but I just want to be friends.

There's a second silence,
and then Murphy says, "Good friends?"
and I say, "Great friends."

"Okay, then," he says.
"That works for me."

And without missing a beat,
he asks me if I want to go over
to the library in Copley Square
this afternoon
and do some sketching, instead.

He says it's great there
because all these old people
are sitting around reading
so they barely move
and they're really fun to draw
because they have a million lines
on their faces.

I tell him I'd love to,
because now that I know
that *he* knows
exactly how I feel about him,

I don't have to worry anymore.

When I Get Off the Phone

My mother wants to know
who it was.
So I tell her.
"Who's Murphy?" she says.
"Just a friend."

"From where?" she wants to know.
"From art class."
"Are you sure he's just a friend?"
she says,
folding her arms across her chest.

"One hundred percent sure," I say.
"If you saw him,
you'd believe me."
"What's that supposed to mean?"
"It means he's not exactly cute."

"Well,
I want to meet him anyway," she says.
"No problem."
"*Before* you go to the library."
"Whatever."

And I head to my room feeling all mixed-up,
because there's a part of me
that resents her for being so nosy,
but another part of me
that's glad she cares.

Mom Meets Murphy

I've never seen her be so friendly
to a boy before.

She's almost acting like he's
a long lost relative or something.

It's sort of sad,
but I guess it's because he's so—

well,
he's so challenged in the looks department.

She doesn't even object when I bring him up
to my room to show him my drawing table.

Even with Zak or Danny,
that would have worried her.

But I guess she figures there's no way
I'd be tempted to fool around with Murphy.

Too bad none of my boyfriends were homely.
I could have gotten away with a *lot*.

At the Library

I'm thinking that I could easily spend
the whole rest of my life
right here
in this peaceful room,

drawing all these ancient faces
and these gnarled hands,
only taking breaks to eat,
and maybe to sleep,

when I glance up from my sketchbook
and see Murphy smiling at me.
"I knew you'd like it here," he whispers,
"'Cause you're a real artist."

This is the first time anyone's ever
called me an artist, let alone a *real* one.
I feel like a whole new part of me
just got born.

On the Bus Home

I end up telling Murphy
that when we bumped into each other
in the museum that day,

I was in the middle
of taking myself on a vacation
without leaving town,

and he says
he can't believe what
an inspired idea that is,

and right away he starts rattling off
all these places I should go
the next time I do it,

like this really funny gallery
he just discovered last week
called the Museum of Bad Art.

He says it's full of these fantastically
awful paintings with names like
Two Trees in Love and *Nauseous*.

But his favorite ones are
Burger on the Beach
and *Sightless Dog with Ear Infection*.

He says
I've just *got*
to see them.

And before I know it,
we're planning a stay-in-town vacation
for *two*.

Painting the Town

The Museum of Bad Art is just as funny
as Murphy said it would be.
Where else you could see
Any Fruit in a Storm
and *Tinkerbell in a Time Tunnel*
on the same wall?

From there, we go to the aquarium,
down on Central Wharf,
to sketch the electric elephant-nose fishes
and the bluestriped grunts.

We start inventing
our own ridiculous names
for every fish that swims by,
and dissolve into hysterics.

Next we go
to the Golden Palace in Chinatown,
and order pan-fried chicken dumplings.
(It turns out they're *Murphy's*
favorite food in the world, too!)

He starts "dubbing in" the voices
of the people sitting at the other tables,
like they're in a foreign movie,
and I can't stop laughing.

After that,
we feed the squirrels in the Public Garden
and Murphy gets one of them
to climb right into his lap
and eat out of his hand.

Then we ride the elevator sixty stories up
to the top of the John Hancock Building
to see how Boston looks
from 740 feet in the air.

And just as the sun
slips into the Charles River,
I realize that I can't remember
a day in my life
when I've had more fun.

And when I turn
to look at Murphy
I see that he's watching *me*
instead of the sunset.

HEADING HOME

Walking with Murphy
through the bone-freezing chill
towards the bus stop,
I start shivering.

And somehow,
when he slips his arm around me
to warm me up,
it feels right.

Righter than anything ever has.

But We're Just Friends

Aren't we?

And that's how I want it to stay.
Don't I?
That's how it has to stay.
Doesn't it?

I mean,
we're talking about *Murphy* here.
He's not exactly boyfriend material.
Is he?

I could never be attracted
to someone like him.
Could I?
That wouldn't make any sense.
Would it?

I mean,
he's *Murphy*.
We're just friends.
And that's all we'll *ever* be.

Right?

I'm Dreaming

I'm dreaming
of the man in *Le Bal à Bougival*,
of him kissing me,
again and again.

I'm dreaming of his lips
sizzling all the cells in my body,
of wishing he would remove
every stitch of my clothes.

I'm dreaming of him
slowly unbuttoning my blouse,
the hundreds and hundreds and hundreds
of buttons on my blouse.

But just as the last one is undone
and he reaches out to do
what my eyes are commanding him to do,
he turns into Murphy.

And in my dream,
this only makes me
want him
more.

His fingers move towards me
in slow motion and I'm burning to know
how his hands will feel
cupping the lace of my bra—

but there's suddenly
this invisible force field between us,
and his palms go flat and white against it,
as if he's a mime.

Murphy looks shocked for a second,
then bewildered,
then he just shrugs with an accepting grin
as my alarm wakes me.

Now I'm lying here,
breathless,
with a tidal wave of confusion
crashing over me.

A Postcard

I step out onto the porch
and notice it lying there
on the welcome mat.

On the picture side
he's drawn a caricature of himself waving,
wearing a Hawaiian shirt,
Bermuda shorts and slinkster cool shades,
with three cameras around his neck.
It says: "Greetings from Boston."
And he's even drawn
a tiny *Le Bal à Bougival* stamp.

On the message side it says:
"Having a wonderful time.
Wish you were here.
Wait a minute.
You *are* here.
And it's a lucky thing for me.
Love,
Murphy"

I take it up to my room
and read it.
Seventeen times.

A Second Look

I just dug out the old sketch
that I did of Murphy
in art class.

It's funny because
I distinctly remember thinking at the time
that I'd really *captured* him.
But looking at it *now*,
I see that it isn't
a thing like him.

I didn't get
that impish gleam
he has in his eyes,
or that kid-like wonder.
And I didn't catch any of his
goofy sense of humor.

And he has this way
of gluing his eyes right onto yours,
and zoning in on you so totally

that he makes you feel like you're
the most fascinating person in the world.
I missed that completely.

It's like I was *looking* at him
that day in class,
but I wasn't really *seeing* him.

I Check My E-mail

There's one from Grace:

Dearest Fee,

*Now we're on Sanibel Island. The seashells here are just
about knee deep! I must have collected at least a million of
them. I decorated a frame with shells for Henry. I made
something for you too, but it's a surprise. I can't wait to
see your sperm panties and show you my tan. I miss you,
but not as much as I miss Henry (no offense).*

Love, Grace

P.S. Met any hot guys?

And one from Rachel:

Fifi dahlink,

*The lifeguard's name is Jason, but it turns out he has a
total babe girlfriend, which is probably a good thing.
Now I don't have to drown anymore. Besides, I'm finally
starting to miss Danny. But not as much as I miss you.
Is that a bad sign? Can't wait to show you my tan and
see your sperm panties. Has it been lonely there? :(
Or did you finally meet Mr. Right? :)*

xxxooo, Racie

**I don't feel like e-mailing
either of them back just now.**

**Maybe tomorrow.
Or the day after.**

An Invitation

I call Murphy to thank him for the postcard.
He says he wishes we could spend
some time together today,
but he has to go Christmas shopping
with his mom.
And then he and his dad are buying a tree.

I'm amazed at how deflated I suddenly feel,
sort of like a day-old helium balloon.
But I tell him it's no problem.
Then he says he knows I'm Jewish,
but would I like to help him
trim his Christmas tree tomorrow?

My stomach does this little flip-flop
and I say,
"How do you know I'm Jewish?"
"Because you didn't invite me
to your Bat Mitzvah in seventh grade,"
he says with a soft laugh.

"Only because I didn't know you," I say,
and when Murphy doesn't reply,
I add,
"Well, I *knew* you,
but I didn't *know* you."
"So, do you want to then?" he asks.

"Sure," I say.

"If your parents won't mind."

"Are you kidding?" he says.

"They're dying to meet you."

And my stomach does another
little flip-flop.

WHEN MURPHY INTRODUCES ME TO HIS PARENTS

His father takes both my hands in his
and beams at me with the warmest eyes.
They're Murphy's eyes.
He says,
"Thank goodness you're here to help us."

The first thing Murphy's mother says
(after "hello" and
"it's so good to meet you") is:
"My son tells me you're Jewish."

"That's right," I say,
while all the blood in my entire body
rushes to my face.

But then she says,
"I am, too,"
with the nicest, most welcoming smile.
It's Murphy's smile.

"I used to have the worst
Christmas tree envy," she says.
"That's probably one of the reasons
I married my husband—
so I'd finally get to have
a tree of my own."

We all laugh at this.

"And *I* get eight extra days of presents,"
Murphy's dad says,
"plus all the chocolate coins I can eat!"

We laugh again
and then they lead me into the living room
to get started.

It's a Beautiful Tree

So tall and full,
with all of its arms
swooping up at the tips
as if to say,
"Ta da!"

The four of us work
through the long afternoon,
sprinkling the boughs with tinsel and
lights and these funny little ornaments
they've been making for years.

And the entire time,
we're singing along with
these great old rock 'n' roll versions
of all the Christmas songs,
and stringing popcorn and drinking eggnog,

and the only thing missing is
the chestnuts roasting on the open fire.
(Well actually,
they've got the fire,
they just don't have the chestnuts.)

The whole scene is so incredibly Hallmark,
so totally Kodak,
so utterly *It's a Wonderful Life*-ish,
that it's absolutely
perfect.

And when Murphy hands me the star
for the top of the tree,
his fingers brush mine,
and this strange little thrill
shoots right up my arm

to my heart.

When We're Done with the Tree

His parents go out to do some errands.
And as soon as the door closes behind them,
I become acutely aware of the fact
that Murphy and I are

alone together.

And that we're standing
dangerously close to some mistletoe
that's dangling from the light
in the hallway.

But Murphy doesn't seem to notice.

He just smiles at me
and asks me if I'd like to
come upstairs
and see his room.

As innocent as anything.

Murphy's Room

The first thing I see
when he swings open his door,
is that he's got
one whole wall
done up like a huge bulletin board.

He's covered it with sketches
and paintings that he's done,
and all these comics
and photos and poems,
and images he's cut out of magazines.

And these headlines from trashy papers,
that say things like:
PSYCHIC LOBSTER EARNS GAMBLER FOUR MILLION!
and TEN PEOPLE VANISH WITHOUT A TRACE
IN PORTABLE TOILET!

Then I notice
a postcard of *Le Bal à Bougival*.
And right there next to it
is a picture of *me!*
The one he drew that day in art class.

And somehow,
seeing it up there
right on Murphy's wall like that,
makes me feel like hundreds of butterflies
are fluttering around inside of me.

I Tell Him How Much I Love His Wall

Especially his psychic lobster headline.
Then we start joking around about pets
and we end up griping about the fact
that neither of us *have* any,
and Murphy sighs and says
that all he wants for Christmas is a dog.

But he says there's no way it'll happen
because his mom's allergic.
And then I tell him *my* mom's allergic too,
and so we marvel over this coincidence
and then we start commiserating about
our tragically dogless lives

and soon we're plotting ways
to earn enough money to buy
a secret golden retriever together
and giggling about how we'll name him Artie
and hide him from our parents
by disguising him as a kinetic sculpture.

And while we're rolling around on the floor
laughing about this,
I come to the sudden
and very startling realization
that all *I* want for Christmas
is Murphy.

!!!

A few minutes later
we're just goofing around,
drawing tattoos on each other's arms,

when this
real slow song
comes on the radio,

and before I even know what's happening,
he grabs hold of my hand, pulls me up,
wraps his arms around me,

and we're dancing,
real slow,
like the song,

and suddenly
this shiver ripples
through every cell in my body—

whoa . . .

224

it's *him*—
my masked man—
Murphy's my masked man!

This Time

When he asks me if I want to go out
to the movies with him tonight,
I say Yes, with a very capital Y.

Yes, I say, Yes!
And when he pulls me to him
and presses his lips to mine

it feels as if
our souls
are kissing.

And it's
exactly like
I used to imagine it

only all that love,
all that need,
is pouring out of *both* of us.

And when we finally stop
to catch our breath,
and I open my eyes,

I notice this one dark curl
hanging down right
in the middle of his forehead

and I think how sexy it looks
and wonder why
I never noticed it before.

Then we press our lips together again,
and I can feel it
down to the tips of my toes.

We Hear the Front Door Opening

But we can't stop kissing.
Maybe we'll *never* stop.
Ever.

But then his mother shouts up the stairs,
"Robin . . ."
And then again, "Robinnn . . ."

We manage to pry our lips apart.
And for half a second I think that maybe
Murphy has a brother I don't know about.

Then
I suddenly remember.
"*You're* Robin!"

"Yeah,"
he says with a wry smile,
"I know."

It's been so many years since
the kids at school have called him that,
that I'd almost forgotten.

"I'm going to call you Robin
from now on," I say,
"If that's okay . . ."

And
he answers
with a kiss.

In the Movie Theater

Robin whispers something to me,
and when his lips
brush against my ear,
all the atoms in my body
start vibrating,

as though I'm a harp
and every single one
of my strings
has just been plucked
at the exact same time.

I don't catch what he says.
But it doesn't matter.
And when our fingers bump
in the popcorn box,
a shower of sparks flies out.

Hair Prayer

His hand's
in my hair.
May he leave it
right there
until April
or May,
near the nape
of my neck
just below
my left ear.
Let it stay
where it is,
right here
in my hair
and not go
anywhere
for a year
and a day.
Better yet,
let it stay
till I'm gray.

DEAR GRACHEL AND RACE,

Merry Xmas! I hope you don't mind that I'm e-ing you both at the same time, but I only have a nanosecond to write because I've got a date with this guy named Robin. Isn't that the most beautiful name in the world? He is definitely my Mr. Right-and-a-half! He's really into art like me and he's funny and smart and when he kisses me, it's so intense it feels like our molecules are practically fusing together!

Last night we went caroling in Louisburg Square. I sort of hummed through the parts about Jesus, but it was so fun. And today, Robin gave me these chubby little pads of paper and I gave him some fancy sketching pencils. So we ended up drawing this great flip book together. It's so cool. Can't wait to show it to you. And my sperm panties, too. (No. I have <u>not</u> shown them to Robin!)

Oops. There's the doorbell. Gotta run.
Love, Fee

By the Charles

The sun's
a big gold coin
floating in an ocean of pink,
behind the lacy silhouettes
of the trees.

We're watching the Citgo sign
splash its neon onto the water,
turning it red,
then blue, then violet,
then red again.

"I love that sign," I say.
"I love *you*," Robin says.
I feel my cheeks
turn the color of the sky.
"I love you, *too*," I say.

Then we kiss
and kiss again
as swirls of the lightest snow
start fluttering down around us,
like tiny frozen feathers.

A Foot of Snow Has Fallen!

We've been sledding
and making snow angels
and having snowball fights,

and building snowmen
and snowwomen
and snowdogs and snowmonsters,

and drawing huge hearts
in the snow
with our initials in them,

and everything's twinkly
and gleaming
and soft.

And if this
was a scene in a movie,
it would definitely be the sappy montage.

Winter Kiss

our cheeks
burning with the cold

the tips of our noses
numb

our icicled lips
bump clumsily

then suddenly
melt together
warming us better
than any cup of steaming cocoa ever could

It's Odd About Kissing

When I first met Dylan
I wanted to kiss him all the time.
But the more I got to really know him,
the less I felt like kissing him.
And it was the same way
with Lou before that.

But with Robin it's the other way around.
The more I get to really know him,
the *more* I want to kiss him.
And his kisses are so powerful
they're almost like kisses
from another planet.

Maybe that's just how it is
when your mind and your body
and your heart and your soul
are in total agreement with each other.
Maybe that's how it is
when it's *real* love.

His Forearms

It's hard to keep my eyes off them,
hard to keep my mind off them,
hard to keep my hands off them
when his sleeves are rolled up.

The curve of them,
where they taper down to his wrists.
That incredibly warm skin,
sprinkled with the silkiest golden brown hairs.

It's hard to keep my fingers from
brushing across them
on the way
to taking hold of his hands.

MORE E-MAIL

Dear Fee,

Hooray! Your bird boy sounds incredible. I'm coming home Saturday (New Year's Eve!) and I'm planning on having just about the most delirious make-out session in history with Henry . But I'm coming over to your house first thing New Year's morning. So you better be ready to tell me all the juicy details!

Love, Grace

P.S. When can I meet him?

Dear Fifi,

Picture me fainting with joy, and then coming to and jumping up and down and shouting YIPPEE!!!! really loud, and then fainting again. Because that's what I did when I got your e about Mr. Robin Right-and-a-half. I'm soooooo happy for you! Arriving home on Saturday afternoon. Breaking up with Danny New Year's Eve. (Well, thinking about it anyway . . .) But, I'll be beating down your door on Sunday morning. I want to know absolutely <u>EVERYTHING!!!!</u>

Love, Rachel

MY NEW YEAR'S RESOLUTION

I, Sophie Stein,
hereby resolve to tell Rachel Ness
and Grace Brody
the true identity of my new boyfriend
on New Year's Day.

No matter what.

And
to not spend one second
between now and then
worrying about
how they're going to react.

(Yeah. Right.)

New Year's Eve

My parents know I'm over here at Robin's.
But what they don't know
is that his parents have gone next door
to a party.

And even if they did,
they wouldn't be worried,
since they still think
we're just friends.

Robin's parents *know*
we're more than friends,
but they said
they trust us implicitly,

by which
I think they meant,
"So don't do anything
we wouldn't want you to do."

And we haven't.

So far.

Shadow Play

We've turned off all the lights
in the living room
to make hand shadows.

We've got this
big flashlight
aimed at the wall.

I make the silhouette of my hand
into a duck.
Robin makes his into a rabbit.

Now my duck kisses his rabbit
And—*POOF!*—it turns into
a turkey.

And for some reason
this strikes us
as hysterically funny.

But you probably had to be there.

More Shadows

I aim the flashlight straight up
at the center of the ceiling.
Robin raises his hand high above it.

Then slowly,
with his fingers outstretched,
he brings it down towards the light.

This makes it look like
the enormous hand of a giant
is clamping down over the room,

till we're
alone together
under a tent of thrilling darkness.

At Midnight

We toast each other
with Perrier
in champagne glasses.

We watch
the ball drop
in Times Square.

Then we sink back
into the cushions of the couch
and kiss the New Year in,

his body pressing
so tightly to mine
that I feel my breath quickening,

my heart
pounding
against his—

But suddenly
the key turns in the lock
of the front door—

and a second later,
when his parents walk into
the living room,

they find us sitting
at opposite ends of the couch,
utterly engrossed in the TV.

On the Drive Home

Robin's dad is giving me
a detailed list
of every New Year's resolution
that he's ever made in his life.

And I'm sitting here
watching all the Christmas lights
drift past the window,
trying my best to listen.

But it's hard,
because I can't stop thinking
about Rachel and Grace and about
how they're both coming over to see me

just a few hours from now.

I Try to Picture It

I try to picture myself
telling them.
I try to hear myself
saying the words.
"You'll never guess
who Robin *really* is."

I try to picture myself saying, "Murphy."
I try to imagine them squealing
and leaping up to hug me,
telling me they always suspected
he was an amazingly neat guy
underneath that dull exterior.

But all I can picture
is Rachel's face going white,
Grace's eyes getting huge.
All I can hear is
Rachel's nervous giggle
and Grace saying, "Oh. My. God."

And all I can think about
is how sick I'm going to feel,
and how hard it will be
not to blurt out, "Aw, come on, guys.
You didn't think I was really *serious*,
did you?"

REUNION

Grace gives Rachel and me each
a pair of outrageously glam sunglasses that
she decorated for us with tiny seashells.

Rachel gives each of us
a bottle of Sky Blue Pink nail polish
and matching Sky Blue Pink lip gloss.

And I give each of them
a pair of sperm panties,
which they absolutely flip out over.

But all of that takes half a minute.
Then they start grilling me
about Robin.

It's funny how you can tell the truth
without actually telling the truth
just by leaving out one little detail.

I tell them
all about how we met
in the museum that day,

and about how
he turned out to be
my masked man.

I even reveal
that he goes
to our school.

I tell them everything.
Except who the heck it is
that I'm *really* talking about.

But no matter how hard I try,
I just can't keep
my New Year's resolution.

When They Finally Leave

I walk
to the basement door,
a storm raging
in my chest.

I reach for the knob,
yank it open,
and gaze down the stairs
through the blur of hot tears,

listening to the silence of the musty dark,
picturing myself
sprawled on the old mattress,
stuffing Hershey's Kisses into my mouth—

Then I shiver,
slam the door shut,
grab my skates
and bolt out of the house.

On Valadon Pond

Skating alone,
round and around,
my thoughts tie themselves
into knots in my head.

What should I do?
Round and around.
How can I tell them?
What will they say?

Memories swirl,
round and around,
of how it felt
when his hand held mine

and we skated alone,
round and around,
on Valadon Pond
together.

SUDDENLY I SEE ROBIN

He's skating towards me
from the edge of the pond,
and when he sees that I'm crying
he just wraps me in his arms
without saying a word.

I feel so totally in love.
And so totally miserable.

When I finally stop crying, he says,
"You haven't told them it's me yet,
have you?"

A quiver runs through me.
How did he know?!
"I'm sorry, Robin," I whisper.

"It's okay, Sophie," he says.
"I'll understand if it has to end."

His words bring
a fresh burst of tears.
"Aw, come on," he says,
with a sad, sweet smile.
"Don't be such a Murphy."

And then
he kisses me.

For the last time?

ANOTHER BUSINESS TRIP

My father smiles and says goodbye
to my mother and me.

But he doesn't kiss us.
Big surprise.

I watch my mother's face
as he climbs into the taxi.

And I suddenly find myself
hugging her.

With all my might.

The Cars Passing By

Why do the shadows
of their headlights,
gliding slowly across my bedroom wall,
make me feel so hollow inside?

Why do the oceany whispers
of their wheels on the road,
drifting near then fading away,
make my chest ache like this?

Why can't I be
in one of those cars
with Robin right now,
zooming away—

far, far away—
from here,
from school,
from tomorrow?

I Hear Footsteps

And then there's a soft knock
on my bedroom door.
Mom slips in and sits on the edge of my bed.

"It's eleven p.m.," she says.
"I tapped. You didn't tap back.
Is something the matter?"

"Yes," I say.
"Everything."
"I know how you feel," she says.

And she looks at me with such sad eyes
that I suddenly find myself
telling her the whole story.

She doesn't really say much,
but it helps to know
she's listening.

And when I get to the part
about Robin being much more than a friend,
she doesn't even get mad.

She just smiles and says, "I can see why."

Tomorrow Is Here

I've been hanging in the girls' bathroom,
hiding out between every class,
waiting for the halls to empty.

But now it's lunchtime.
I can't avoid him
forever.

I feel so scared.
Of how I'll act
and of what I'll say when I see him.

And of how *he'll* act
and of what *he'll* say
when he sees *me*.

And of how Rachel and Grace
and everyone else will act
and of what they'll all say,

to my face and behind my back,
if they see Robin and me,
Murphy and me,

together.

I Slink into the Cafeteria

And scan the multitudes.
It only takes me a second to find Robin,
sitting alone at a table by the window.

He doesn't see me.

But Rachel and Grace do.
They wave me over.
I force a smile and wave back.

But I stay where I am.

Rachel calls out my name.
Robin looks up and sees me.
He smiles.

But only with his eyes.

Is everyone
in the entire cafeteria
looking at me?

Or is it just my imagination?

I try to lift my feet
but they feel like they've been
nailed down to the linoleum.

My body's getting ready to fly apart.

I want to scream.
I want to run away.
I want to—

No! I don't.

I race over to Robin,
sit down across from him
and take hold of his hands.

Robin's smiling with more than his eyes now.

He's smiling through and through.
And I am, too.
Because everything's going to be all right.

Sometimes I just *know* things.

ABOUT THE AUTHOR

Before becoming a writer, SONYA SONES *taught animation in schools all across the country, worked as a still photographer, and edited movies in Hollywood. Her acclaimed first book,* Stop Pretending: What Happened When My Big Sister Went Crazy, *was a finalist for the* Los Angeles Times *Book Prize and the winner of a Christopher Award, the Claudia Lewis Poetry Award, and the Myra Cohn Livingston Poetry Award. It was also an American Library Association Best Book for Young Adults and a Top Ten Quick Pick for Reluctant Young Adult Readers.*

Here's what Ms. Sones says about the genesis of What My Mother Doesn't Know: *"My first book,* Stop Pretending, *is autobiographical. Toward the end of that book, which is also written in poetry, there are some poems about my first love, a boy named John. I had such a good time writing about those first feelings of overwhelming passion, that I knew I wanted to delve into them more deeply. That's when the poems for* What My Mother Doesn't Know *began bubbling to the surface. Unlike the poems in* Stop Pretending, *these poems are definitely not autobiographical. Especially not the embarrassing ones."*

Ms. Sones lives with her husband and two children near the beach in California. Visit her Web site at www.sonyasones.com.